B

This Walker book belongs to:

_____

_____

_____

This is a book about forces.
A force is something that makes an object move,
stop moving or change direction. We can apply
a force by pushing or pulling.

For Kate, Louise and Denise – M. J.
For Mum and Dad – R. J.

First published 2018 by Walker Books Ltd, 87 Vauxhall Walk, London SE11 5HJ
This edition published 2019
2 4 6 8 10 9 7 5 3 1
Text © 2018 Martin Jenkins
Illustrations © 2018 Richard Jones

The right of Martin Jenkins and Richard Jones to be identified as author and illustrator respectively of this work
has been asserted by them in accordance with the Copyrights, Designs and Patents Act 1988.

This book has been typeset in Kreon
Printed in China

British Library Cataloguing in Publication Data: a catalogue record for this book is available from the British Library.
ISBN 978-1-4063-8270-9
www.walker.co.uk

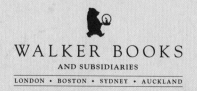

WALKER BOOKS
AND SUBSIDIARIES
LONDON • BOSTON • SYDNEY • AUCKLAND

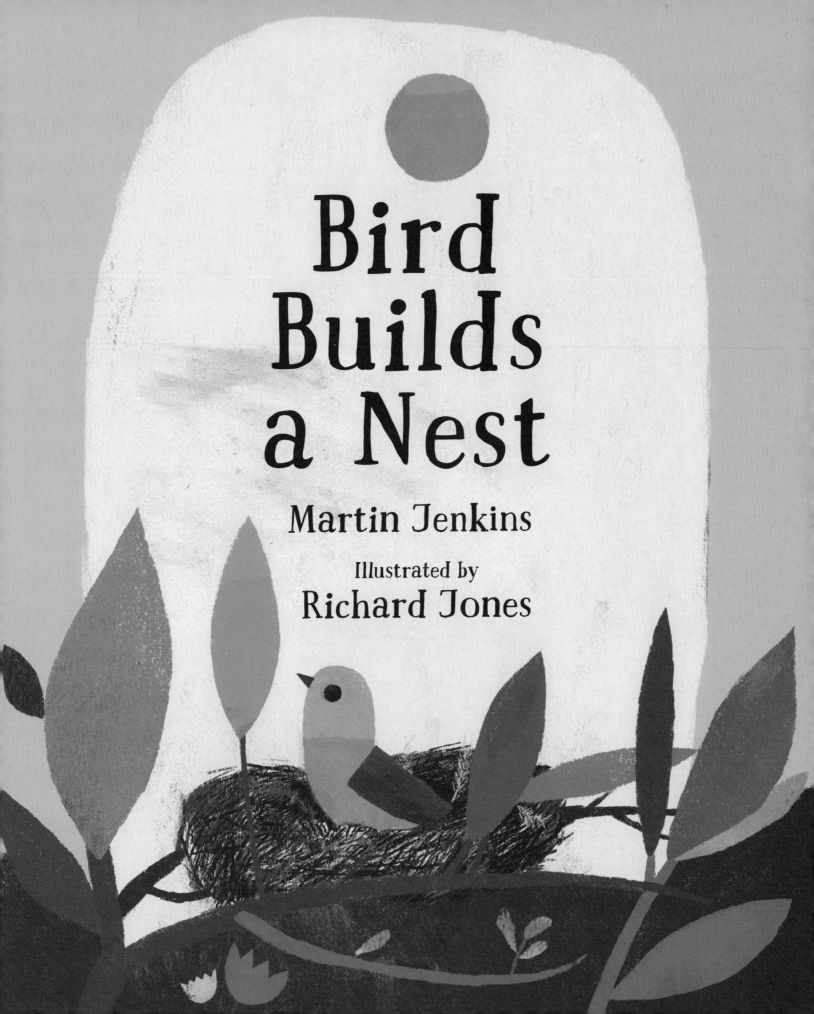

Bird
Builds
a Nest

Martin Jenkins

Illustrated by
Richard Jones

It's a beautiful day!
Bird is up early –
she's got a lot to do.

First she needs some breakfast.
What she wants is a nice, juicy ...

worm.

Bird is getting ready to pull the worm. When you pull something, you are applying a force towards you.

Bird pulls hard, but
the worm pulls back.

The stronger something
is, the more force
it can apply.

It's a big worm,
and it's strong.

Too strong for Bird.

Ah. This one's better.

It's smaller and not as strong. Delicious!

Now she can get on with her work.

She's not looking for worms now.

She needs twigs. Lots of twigs.

This one's too
heavy.

The more something weighs, the more force you need to lift it.
Bird isn't strong enough to apply enough force to lift the twig.

And so is this one.

All of these will do fine.

Bird can carry:
this quite large twig

or two medium-sized twigs

or three or four small twigs.
But sometimes she can find it tricky fitting
that many in her beak at once.

She's building her nest.
It's not quite finished though.
Carefully, she pushes a twig into the side of
the nest and pulls its end back out.

Pushing and pulling, she gets all
the twigs in place.

When you push something, you are applying a force away from you.

She works for hours,

fetching and carrying,

flying backwards and forwards,

pushing and pulling.

Sometimes she drops a twig, but it doesn't matter.

Things fall to the ground because of a force called gravity.
You can't see gravity, but it's everywhere.

She's looking for softer
things now. Dried grass and feathers.
They're very light. She can carry
lots of these at once.

She tucks them into place.

Turning round and round,
pushing with her whole body,

she makes a snug little cup,
smooth and soft on the inside.

Ready and waiting.

Can you guess what for?

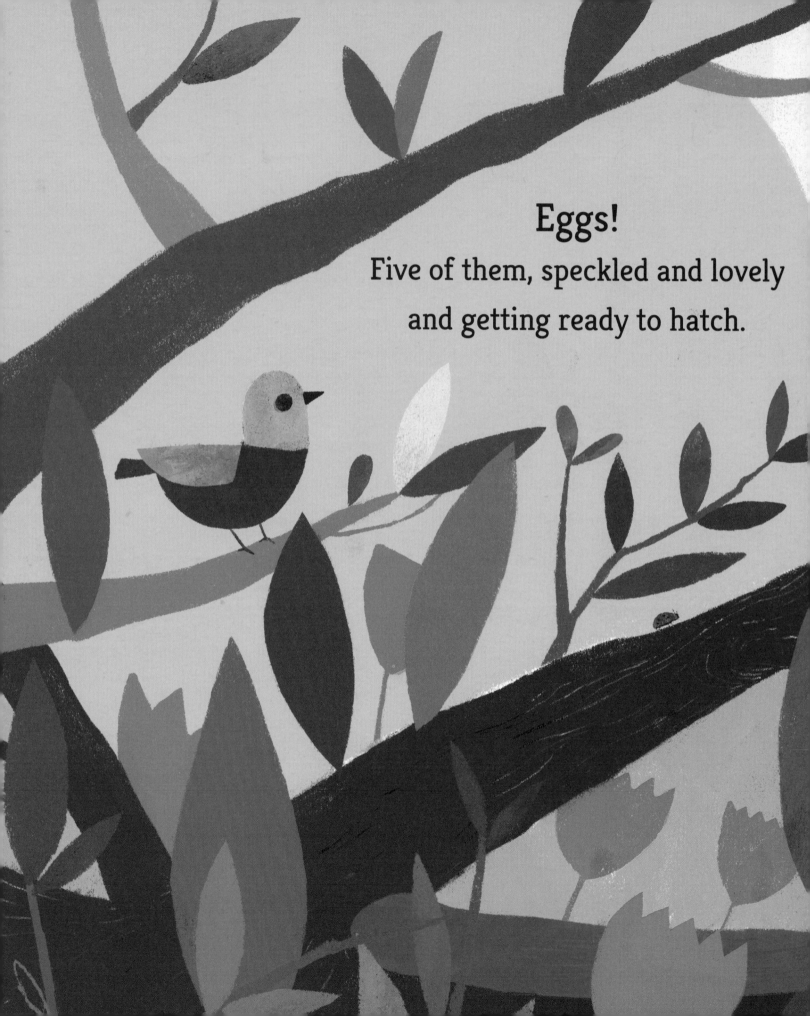

Eggs!
Five of them, speckled and lovely
and getting ready to hatch.

THINKING ABOUT
PUSHING AND PULLING

Try an experiment with forces. Find a ping pong ball.

Now make a ball the same size out of modelling clay. Lift one up in each hand.

Which one is easier to lift? Can you think why?

How many ping pong balls do you think you could lift at once?

How many modelling clay balls?

Now hold the ping pong ball and the clay ball as high as you can
and let them go at the same time.

Do you think one of them will fall faster?

Can you see if one hits the ground first?

INDEX
Look up the pages to find out about forces. Don't forget to look up both kinds of word, this kind – and **this kind.**

More Science Storybooks:

ISBN: 978-1-4063-8252-5

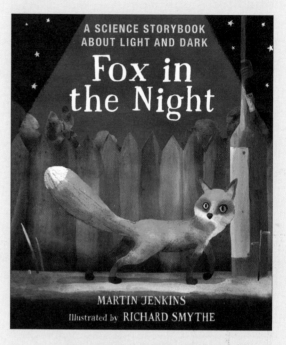

ISBN: 978-1-4063-7975-4

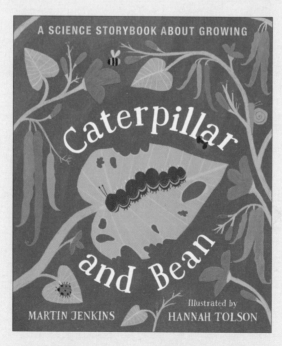

ISBN: 978-1-4063-5516-1